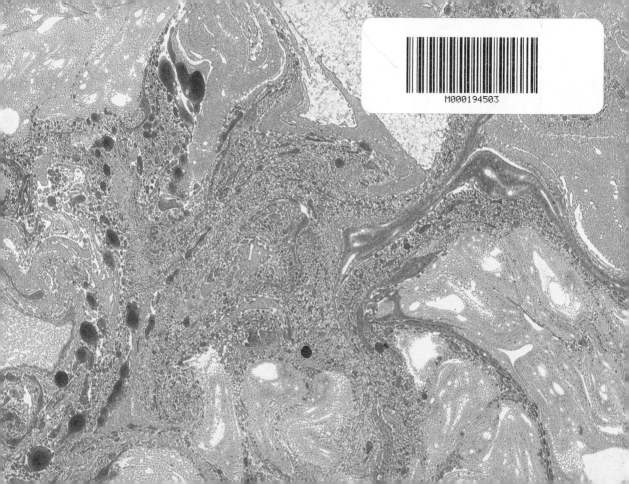

Graham Clarke

ENGELSKMANN I LOFOTEN

A NORWEGIAN SKETCHBOOK

J.W. Cappelens Forlag A.S

GRAHAM CLARKE
White Cottage, Green Lane
BOUGHTON MONCHELSEA
MAIDSTONE KENT.
ENGLAND

ENGELSKMANN I LOFOTEN
A NORWEGIAN SKETCHBOOK

ENGELSKMANN I LOFOTEN

A NORWEGIAN SKETCHBOOK

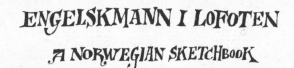

Copyright © 1996 Graham Clarke

First published in Norway in 1996 by J.W. Cappelens Forlag A·S, Oslo

Reproduced and printed by Tangen Grafiske Senter As Drammen, Norway

ISBN 82-02-15967-9

SVOLVÆR, LOFOTEN

THE Harbour of SVOLVÆR is infact an ARCHIPELAGO
Islands & Islets by the dozen. Many being interconnected by bridges
and causeways.
Fishing has been the chief activity here for at least 1000 years.

Many places in the world are
referred to as 'Magical' and
some I have visited.
When applied to these islands
it could be true, they are
certainly the most beautiful
I have ever seen.

MORE
PROBABLY

INTRODUCING
ODD the COD

p.9

I am here in LOFOTEN at suggestion of our VERY good friend DAG RANDULff of STAVANGER, he is full of GOOD IDEAS that enable ME to BECOME better aquainted with his Beautiful Country. This trip SEEMS to be his best idea yet.

ACCORDINGly this book is dedicated to him.

"GOD DAG"

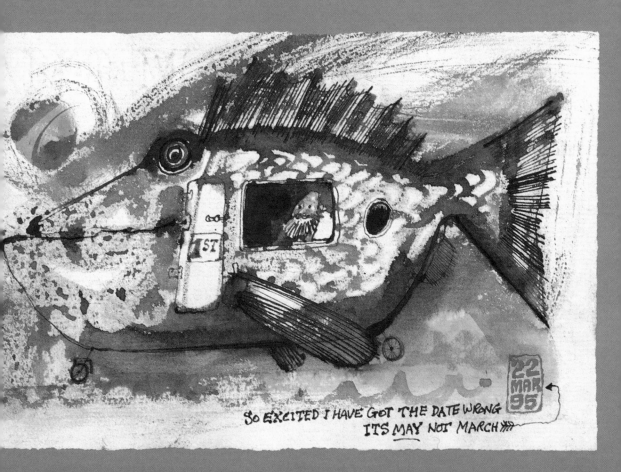

SO EXCITED I HAVE GOT THE DATE WRONG
ITS MAY NOT MARCH

THE Bicycle

"Easy to Hire, Difficult to Ride"

the bike was cheap even for Norway. I was shown
how to operate the **LOCK** Not that anything is ever
stolen. It was a Ladies Bike (No Problem). N. GEARS
- a problem. My problem - Back Pedal Brake.

APOLOGY Nº1

The above drawing makes the Machine look
like a motorcycle - it was not of course.
perhaps it is a sub-conscious artistic
expression regarding it's weight.

what does this man
expect for Kr.10 a
day?

VÅGAN

LOW Tide near VÅGE
church. A Settlement he
was once the most
NORTHERLY TOWN in the
WORLD.

13.

VERY ODD

ODD seems a very odd name to us ENGLISH. I now know three Odds.

1. ODD Number ONE has a second hand book shop and half a pub in STAVANGER also a fine VIKING MOUST-ACHE. He insists on giving me lovely old books and free beer – I like him.

2. ODD Number 2 also a Very kind Man, he is an architect and responsible for most of the fine new buildings in ÅLESUND, he gives me SALMON.

* Although well inside the ARCTIC CIRCLE LOFOTEN escaped the ICE AGE as it was so far out to sea and already enjoying the benefits of the Gulf Stream.
As a consequence its marvellous rugged mountains of ancient formation were not smoothed off. GOOD.

➤ * OR MOST of it anyway.

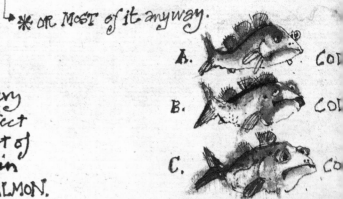

A. COD

B. COD

C. COD

P.15

ODDS (CONTINUED)

3. ODD Number three we met in SIRDAL high in the mountains of Southern NORWAY. He keeps more than **40** husky DOGS and took us up into the wilderness in deep deep snow with more snow falling. We fell off the three sledges and got lost, it was a little exciting. He is probably a TROLL.

TROLLS — See Page 36

linguistic note for Norway ──→

A Fellow artist in the KUNSTNERHUSET is LEIF ANDERSSON an almost too cheerful SWEDE. MY explanation that a Swede should behave like any other breed of TURNIP produced. No improvement in his behaviour.

Today he leaves at 8am on the fastboat for Narvik. [NORWICK] ←

IN honour of his departure the sun comes out and SPRING arrives.

"LEIF LEAVES & THE LEAVES ARRIVE"

SWEDE = SVENSKE
SWEDE = KÅLROT

THIS SEAGULL is No Fool. A WARM CHIMNEY & a Cosy NEST tucked out of the prevailing winds, & out of the reach of the numerouse CATS.

Warm Weather is here : Good for Artists and Baby Seagulls.

AND

HAYMAKE EGG

Note the very NICE [4] FISH Scale Roof ➤

Slates cut carefully. 10/10

QUESTION
Why were the Seagull Eggs on the FISH COUNTER in the shop and not with the hens eggs?

19.

GUNNAR BERG
1863 - 1893
LOFOTENS MALER.

ON MY early MORNING walk around
MY small island. I am suddenly
CONFRONTED by this dignified
GENTLEMAN. He died aged ONLY
30 years of age poor fellow, but
WARRANTED a nice statue. I
assumed he must be a sailor or
FISHERMAN, but NO a MALER
is a PAINTER. ARTISTS are
MUCH RESPECTED in this Little
Town and have been welcomed
here for 100 years, as indeed
I have been.

I Discover later that Gunnar Berg is a very well
known artist. Famous for his " BATTLE of TROLLFJORD
Paintings in SVOLVAER TOWN HALL.

APOLOGY No. 2

The writing and lettering in this little book is rather untidy as you have noticed I am sure. There are 3 main reasons.

① I made the book myself and it does not open very well.

② Much of it was written on board ship or boat.

③ My writing is always untidy anyway.

G.C.

Kabelvåg another ancient fishing community and formerly the most important in Lofoten. Vågen which now gives its name to this Kommune was once the most Northerly town in the World.

I was told that Kabelvåg gave its name to "Cabbilaud" the French name for Codfish.

oui c'est vrai

23.

Page 25.

The Quay at Kabelvåg →→→
Warehouses, rocks and a nice
old sailing boat.
The Weather is Not at all COLD
but RAIN IS ON the Way, Cloud
makes the ISLANDS offshore dissapear suddenly
and I get Wet riding home.

27.

TORSK (COD) are caught by the million in February and a large proportion are hung up to dry on massive 'A' frame racks. Exposed to all weathers until June when they are shut away to warmer climes presumably to be much enjoyed. Up here however they are shunned by gulls from above and cats below. Yes, they do smell a little. The heads are tied in great bunches and hung separately.

Tied in pairs and hooked over tails.

STOCKFISH TO YOU.

TØRRFISK EVEN THE CATS WON'T TOUCH IT...

Tilly &
dià thn

31.

NOTE
NO HORNS
ON HELMET.

VIKINGS liked these Islands too, at BORG on VESTVÅGØY was found the largest BUILDING in All NORDIC Countries. Now a fine Museum.

It's NEST BUILDING time for the Seagulls, this seems to bring out the more quarrelsome side of their nature.
I was enjoying the sunshine sitting on a Rock eating an apple and a seagull came to watch me. It seemed only polite to offer him the apple core core. He was most grateful and ate the lot while defending his prize from his neighbours, NOT AN EASY TASK.

Page 33

From the **KUNSTNERHUSET** [ARTISTS HOUSE] Kitchen Window

where I am staying

Is a fine view of SVINØYA (the island of PIGS?)   THE RED BUILDING IS NOT A CHURC
BUT AN OLD HOUSE WITH its OWN
LOOKOUT! Built by Sailor or Ship
owner
MR. Berg?

MR. & MRS. EIDERDUCK

Everyone loves these
nice ducks and they
are particularly
pleased with them
here in LOFOTEN.
They don't seem to
quack but make a
gentle and slightly
surprised "OOOOO?"

P.35

P. 37

Behind SVOLVÆR is a great black
Mountain [except when covered in
snow which is probably most of the
year] Just below the summit is
a famous rock formation
SVOLVÆRGEITA – 'GOAT MOUNTAIN.'
Foolhardy Mountaineers have been
known to jump from one horn to another

* MOST CODFISH have very little sense
of humour — it's a well known fact.
However the ODD COD can occasionally
produce a little SMILE......
BUT ONLY IF YOU TELL HIM A REALLY GOOD JOKE.

SMUDGE ➤➤➤ Warehouses o

BUKKADAUEN
Island. ▲ E NOT A

41.

This Company appears to own Most of the ISLAND I am staying on.

SVINØYA

L. BERGS A/S SØNNER

ETABL. 1828

A SVIN ON HIS ØYA

P.43

SVOLVÆR øøøø ÅÅÅÅ

The Islands forming
the eastern arm of the
harbour, Svinøya (Pig
Island, Gunnar Holmen
(Gunnar Bergs own isle
and Kjeøya are joined
together by causeway
and to the town by
a bridge. The small
island of Lamholmen
has a bridge now too
and a fine new
hotel.
* Sheeps Island.

I am NOT used to drawing Boats
With two sharp ends.

REPAINTING AT KABELVÅG

POSSIBLE SVOLVAER WOODCUTS. →

DRIED COD/SALT COD

These are two quite distinct and different methods of preserving fish although the end results in the cooking pots of the Mediterranean might well be similar. Dried Cod [TØRRFISK] the product presented earlier in this book and is called STOCK by the time it arrives in Italy where it is much appreciated. Salt cod is packed when fresh in vast quantities of salt and when it gets to Portugal or Spain is called BACALAO. I think

This is Page N° 47 please return to P. 39 take note of SVOLVÆR GEITA then these Potatoes.

...WITH POTATOES ARRANGED IN SVOLVÆR MANNER.

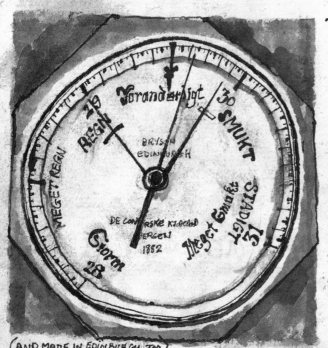

Vorander lgt
REGN
219
30
SMUKT
MEGET REGN
BRYSON
EDINBURGH
STADIGT
31
DE CONTORSKE KLOBAB
BERGEN
1882
MEGET GMOKE
Gtorm
28

(AND MADE IN EDINBURGH TOO)
OLD BAROMETER ON SVINØYA - IN THE RECENTLY OPENED
RESTAURANT.

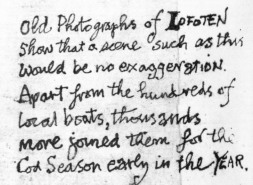

Old Photographs of **LOFOTEN**
Show that a scene such as this
would be no exaggeration.
Apart from the hundreds of
local boats, thousands
more joined them for the
Cod Season early in the YEAR.

Note:- FOR SOME REASON
TWO MEN IN A ROWING
BOAT ARE ALREADY
COMING HOME AGAIN.

Page 49.

A Perfect one-house island ➤➤➤
at the eastern end of Svolvaer
harbour. The dog barks at
me across the water, with my
bag and bicycle maybe he thinks
I am the new postman.

* NOTE The word "Daft" means Stupid or Silly
I see in my little dictionary the NORWEGIAN
word is "Dum".

51.

COOKERY IN fishing COMMUNITIES

Where fish is available in abundance (at almost no cost) as in communities such as this, it is rarely treated to complicated cookery. It is much enjoyed and appreciated however even though cooked so simply. The use of herbs, spices, wine, cream and even pepper and salt seem to be minimal.

AN OLD TIMER outside his RORBU ROBOR.

A RORBU ROBOR is a shed or cabin for use by FISHERMEN. Half built over the water on stilts [see the pictures] the boat can be moored right alongside.

I don't know what this man is doing with a big stick in a tub but I am sure he does.

Across the water to Berg's racks of drying fish: I was prepared for this type of scene before my arrival, having seen photographs of men clambering up the frames.

I was surprised however by the hug bunches of Cods Heads also drying hanging from the Long horizontal poles, their destiny must be gastronomic but its difficult to imagine how they might be used.

"Thankyou ODD"
(ARTIST)

what about Soup you fool?

OR FISH MEAL?

Page 55

ON the ISLAND of SVINØYA near this scene ⟫⟫⟫⟶ and close to Gunnar Bergs statue is an extraordinary Family Grave.

FAMILIE BERG GRAVSTED 18??

THE ISLAND of LITLMOLLA SEEN ⟫⟫⟶ through the arch of Gunnar Bergs' Fish Drying Racks.

Just another CODFISH

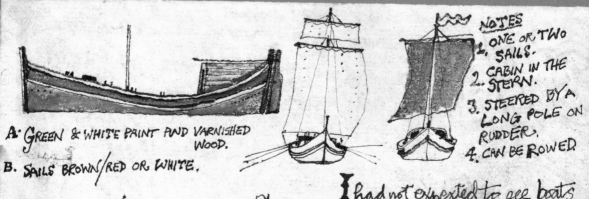

A. GREEN & WHITE PAINT AND VARNISHED WOOD.

B. SAILS BROWN/RED OR WHITE.

NOTES
1. ONE OR TWO SAILS.
2. CABIN IN THE STERN.
3. STEERED BY A LONG POLE ON RUDDER.
4. CAN BE ROWED

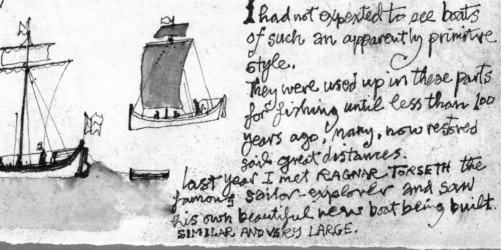

I had not expected to see boats of such an apparently primitive style.

They were used up in these parts for fishing until less than 100 years ago, many, now restored sail great distances.

Last year I met RAGNAR TORSETH the famous sailor-explorer and saw his own beautiful new boat being built. SIMILAR AND VERY LARGE.

NORDLANDSBÅT Design unchanged for 1000 years.

THe white Building to the right
of centre is a fine old warehouse
on SVINØYA full of relics of
fishing and sailing and the
many trades associated with
them. It has just opened as
a restaurant, and very nice
too.

It's NOT GOING to get DARK TONIGHT
OR any other night until SOME TIME
in July or August. But the SUN has
gone behind the MOUNTAIN to tell
us its evening. An old man rows
(facing the 'wrong' way) slowly across
the glassy waters.
He appears to be in no hurry - neither are
we.

TO THE SEA

P.61

I have four NORWEGIAN HATS of which I am very proud.

1.

As worn by KING OLAV [made in SWEDEN]

2.

ØSTERDALSLUE "Very Elegant" with internal ear flaps.

3.

Purchased from the hat maker at the SAUESANKING (Sheep Roundup) in SIRDAL.

4.

Bought in BERGEN Fish Market. [KNITTED]

A Fishermans house, ~~Robur~~ RORBU and boat on SVINØYA. Today, Thursday 25th May is a NATIONAL HOLIDAY so the flag flies proudly.

QUITE right too.

Even more special is 17th MAY Even more flags and even more fish eaten too I expect.

NOTE FOR the information of any kind person wishing to add to this small collection – my hat size is **58**. "thank you."

58

Fish drying in
the rain »—→
?

Svolvaer and the surrounding area will become
the setting for one of my largest etchings.
I hope to begin this later in the year.

Sailing Past Gunnarholmen

The Dramatic Island in the background is SKROVA a unique fishing community determined to work in the OLD FASHIONED way. I wanted to go there, a ferry boat calls in once a day to drop you off and *may* call into pick you up in the evening...

A Last Look [for this visit] at my favourite island at the Eastern entrance to SVOLVÆR HARBOUR, this "notorious" stretch of water is called KVALBAKKEN.

It's calm enough today which is good as this evening I leave on the Coastal Ferry. The dog does not bark.

Am I now accepted as a Local person?

OR MAYBE NOT.

ODD

No, the dog is having a little sleep.

P. 67

29 MAY 95

"Velkommen Ombord"

TROMS FYLKES
DAMPSKIBSSELSKAP
3 Days on the Coastal Ferry
Down to Bergen.

and very
nice too...

Nice old figurehead on KONG HARALD.

FAMOUS MOUNTAIN with a **HOLE** in it.

↑ TORGHATTEN

SEVEN SISTERS

HURTIGRUTENMALERI

Views through the
window. [PORTHOLE]

SOUTH FROM
SvOLVÆR to BERGEN
3 DAYS ON the WONDERFUL HURTIGRUTEN

N

W

E

SOUTH

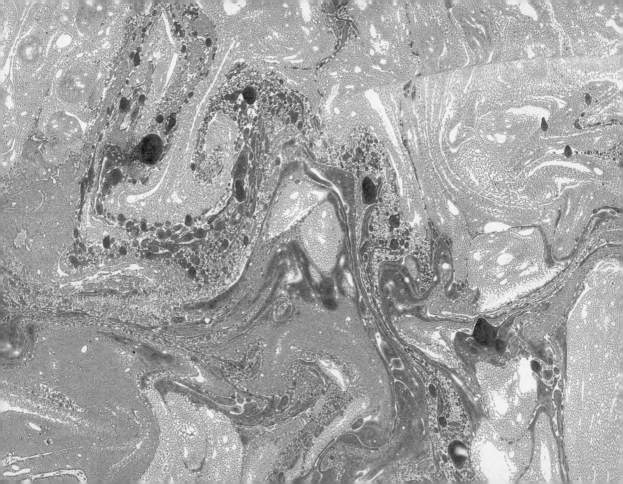